Dear J~~~~~~~~~~~ —
You all are _God's_
gift to me and Grandmother!
We thank Him for all the
joy and happiness you bring
to our lives.

God loves you sor much!
We pray that you will
experience Him and His love
daily. _Seek Him with all
your hearts._ He is seeking _You!_

Yours in Jesus' love,
Granddad

December 2020

GRANDDAD'S
ANIMAL
ADVENTURES

Granddad's Animal Adventures

Stephen Scott Nelson

Stephen S Nelson

Contents

*This book is dedicated to my
grandchildren.*

*It is my prayer that each of you will find
a personal
relationship with your loving Creator.*

He is looking for you!

*Then we, your people, the sheep of
Your pasture, will continually thank
You. We will tell coming generations
of Your praiseworthy acts.
Psalm 79:13 NET*

Acknowledgements

I thank God for revealing Himself to me through His incredible creation. He loved me and wanted me to find Him. At the age of eighteen I came to know God personally and my life was radically changed. He gets all the credit!

My wife, Danelle, patiently supported my writing this book with her wise insights and edits. She has been God's gift to me for 45 years. Thank you sweetheart! You are the love of my life!

Thank you to my dear children, Scott, Whitney, Julie, Matthew, Stephanie, Grace, and Merry, and their spouses, especially David, who helped me with the layout at all hours. They prayed for me and encouraged me to persevere over the many months of this project. I love each one of you so much!

To my dear mother, Alice Turnage Nelson. I appreciate your quality editing. You have done so much more than that. You have raised a son who will attempt great things because you have been my #1 fan! I love you!

My granddaughter, Jasper Newton, who edited my manuscript with precision and great skill. You are mature way beyond your years. Thank you so much!

To my many faithful friends who prayed for me and stood with me to see this book come to fruition. Thank you!

Introduction

Granddad's Animal Adventures

As a young boy, I spent hours in the forest exploring with my friends and their dogs. My family lived in the mountains outside of Asheville, North Carolina. Right behind our house was the door to discovering this interesting world of living creatures. We had numerous adventures together where we encountered a wide variety of animals, as well as various insects. We would collect anything that moved, even the dead ones, and bring them home as our prized treasures. It was exciting! We "rescued" baby rabbits after our dogs found them and ran off their mother. Then we would bring them home and attempt to keep them alive feeding them warm milk from an eye dropper. Unfortunately, we were usually unsuccessful, and the poor rabbits died and went on to rabbit heaven. I still remember how my brother and I felt sad when they died. We sincerely attempted to keep these little creatures alive. Taking baby rabbits and possums home, and trying to raise them, was the kind of thing adventurous young boys did back then. We began to learn about life and death, the circle of life, from these animals. All God's creatures are born and later they will die.

All of us humans have a birthday and eventually we will die too. That is normal. It has been this way since the beginning of time. So why are we afraid of something that happens to everyone? Maybe we are afraid because we do not know where we will go after we die. Later we will talk more about how you can know where you are going after you die and not be afraid. But for now, let me continue telling you about my adventures with animals when I was a kid, as well as a few crazy stories as an adult.

There is something spiritual to be learned from being around plants and animals. It only makes sense that we learn more about God through nature. After all, He created everything! He designed every tree, shrub, insect, turtle, flower, and fish. They reflect the beauty, wisdom, and power of their Maker. My adventures, some of which were surprising and abnormal, helped make me the person I am today. My hope is that they will help you appreciate and enjoy all of God's creatures a little more. It's also my desire for you to have a greater appreciation for the One who created you, since **you are the most valuable of all God's creatures!**

It was through these encounters with God's universe, that He revealed Himself to me. He wanted me to find Him. The word "revelation" means, to reveal something hidden or disclose something unknown. Your parents revealed to you how to feed yourself when you were a baby, how to tie your shoes as a child, or how to use the computer or drive a car. Your teacher helped you understand Algebra or find the theme of a story. You needed their help to understand.

They revealed things to you that you did not know. In the same way, God's revelation is when He communicates a divine truth about Himself. He often reveals Himself in a dramatic way! The Bible says that one-way God *revealed* Himself to us through His creation,

"For since the creation of the world His invisible attributes, His eternal power and divine nature, have been clearly seen, being understood through what has been made." Romans 1:18

Trout Fishing on the Chattahoochee River

God loves you and wants you to find Him. He wants you to begin a personal relationship with Him. When we are born, we do not have this relationship because we are naturally selfish. This selfishness is called sin. God is perfect (holy) and cannot have a relationship with selfish people, even though He loves all of us and wants us to experience Him. We must have a second birth, a spiritual birth, to begin this relationship with God.

""Jesus replied, "I tell you the solemn truth, unless a person is born from above, he cannot see the kingdom of God." John 3:3 NET

We will talk more about how you can have this second birth later in the book. Keep reading!

Now I will tell you some true stories of how God was looking for me. He wanted me to find Him. He was *not hiding* from me. He wants you to find Him too! He promises,

"You will seek Me and find Me when you search for Me with all your heart." (Jeremiah 29:13)

Let the animal adventures begin!

Adventure 1: A Turtle Or A Rock?

One of our favorite things to do as young boys (5 to 8 years old), who lived in the mountains of North Carolina, was to bring home turtles like the Eastern Box Turtle in the photograph above. Many box turtles were transplanted from their natural environment in the woods to our "Turtle Hotel," the chicken wire pen we made behind our house. The turtles did not have to crawl far to visit with their fellow turtles, and they enjoyed all the earthworms and blackberries they could eat without having to work for them. We made sure they never went hungry. Have you ever watched a box turtle eat an earthworm? If you have, you will never forget how seriously the turtle takes it! Maybe you can watch a video of a turtle eating an earthworm on YouTube. Eventually, all the box turtles we captured either escaped their pen or were released. No harm, no foul. It was great fun for little children who loved to explore. As young children, our hearts were touched by these encounters with God's creatures. We were never the same afterwards!

One warm sunny day in June, my friends and their dogs came to our house to get me and explore the forest. We went straight down the hill and into the White Pine and Hemlock forest in search of turtles. We ran free and breathed in the clean mountain air. After a few hours, we were tired of going up and down the hills, so we decided to stop and rest. I decided to sit down on a large rock. The rock moved! I jumped up, frightened and trying to understand what was going on. When my buddies and I realized it was really a large tortoise, we laughed and talked about how we had never seen such a huge turtle. No, we did not attempt to take him home to join the box turtles behind our house.

Have you noticed that sometimes things are not what they seem to be? This snapping turtle was not a rock. He, or she, looked like a rock to a tired little boy, but he was a living creature. What a surprise. I'm sure the turtle was surprised too when I sat on him!

A Lesson to Learn: *God Wants To Surprise You With New Things.*

The rock did not magically change into a turtle. God made the turtle years ago when its mother laid an egg in the ground. What changed that day was my understanding. I was educated when he moved.

In the same way, we may go to the doctor because we think we have a serious illness, only to be told that it is just a cold and we do not need to worry. The doctor assures us that, even though we have pain in our stomach right now, she has some medicine that will make us get well. We are surprised and happy. Our understanding of the problem changed, and it was a good surprise. Of course, sometimes surprises are unpleasant, or even difficult, and they make us sad or afraid.

Snapping Turtle with his head pulled inside. Could he look like a rock to you?

God always wants to surprise you in many good ways. He wants to answer your prayers. He wants to give you wisdom, peace, and courage and to show you His love each day. He wants to surprise you with His peace when you are worried. He wants to give you wisdom when you do not know the right thing to do. He wants you to show kindness to others who might hurt or irritate you, even your brother or sister. God wants to surprise you, but there is something you must do first. You need to call on Him – to ask Him for help. If you do not ask, you won't discover what He wants to show you. On the other hand, if you do ask for His help, trusting Him to answer, He promises to do so! Here is His promise,

"Call on me in prayer and I will answer you. I will show you great and mysterious things which you still do not know about." Jeremiah 33:3 NET

Is there something that you need help understanding? Then ask God to show you. He loves you, and He will answer you and show you great and mighty things you do not know about!

Adventure 2: Petting Tom

Did you know that not all turkeys are created equal? It is true. Domestic turkeys are the turkeys which are raised on farms and appear on your dinner table at Thanksgiving. They usually have white feathers, are not very smart, and they are in great need of exercise. You see, they never have to travel and hunt for the food they eat. Their food is provided for them by the farmer. Their life is one of standing around, eating, drinking, and getting fat. Farmers want to raise big, fat turkeys to sell to us and make more money. Nobody wants to buy a skinny turkey!

Wild turkeys, on the other hand, are smart, strong, and can run and fly extremely fast. I have watched them fly from the ground up into trees eighty feet in the air. Wild turkeys can run up to 25mph, which is faster than most humans. They can also fly 55mph for up to a mile, the average speed limit for cars on the highway! I have hunted turkeys in the fields and forests of South Carolina and Georgia for years. When I went hunting, the turkey usually eluded me and lived to see another day. On my drive home, I would stop by the grocery store to buy one of those frozen, not-so-smart turkeys, that never saw a forest. It made me feel better about myself when I provided some food for the family. After all, what proud hunter wants to come home empty handed after spending hours in the woods?

Do you see the beard on the tom in the photo above?

The female turkey is called a hen, and since they lay the eggs to make more turkeys, they are illegal to shoot. The female is smaller.

The male turkey is larger and is called a tom. They have a "beard," which is a clump of hair growing out of their chest. His head is reddish to grey-blue, while the hens have duller feathers and a grayish head.

The tom can also puff his feathers out in what is called a strut, while usually making a drumming sound and a loud gobble. Okay, now that you know some important facts about wild turkeys, let me tell you about my encounter with a peculiar Tom.

To fully appreciate my story, it is imperative that you understand that a wild turkey also has excellent eyesight. The slightest movement a hunter makes can be seen several hundred yards away. That is why the turkey hunter wears camouflage and sits very still. He may even use a decoy (a fake turkey) to fool the tom he into coming to him. In nature, the hen will usually go to the tom. The hunter is attempting to reverse the way God created turkeys to act, by calling the gobbler into him. The hunter calls the Tom using various devices (wooden boxes, slate, and small reeds that fit in the mouth), all named "turkey calls."

Now on to my encounter with Tom. I love to run. One of my favorite trails, when I lived in Canton, Georgia, was along the Etowah River behind Cherokee High School. The trail follows the river, going over a few small foot bridges that cross gurgling brooks with steep hills rising from the river's edge. There are also some cool rock cliffs that you must squeeze by to keep from falling in the raging waters.

One morning I ran down the trail a few miles, my mind lost in the beautiful scenery. As was my custom, I was praising God for what my eyes and ears were enjoying, as well as praying for the needs of my family and friends. I returned on the same trail with the river a few feet to my right and cliffs immediately to my left. I crossed a small stream and gazed ahead a few hundred feet where I saw a large black thing in the narrow path. As I ran closer, I recognized it as a wild turkey. Knowing it would fly away or take off running, I decided to walk and see how close I could get. I was surprised that Tom stayed on the trail. I moved closer in disbelief. Was it real? Was the turkey alive? I cautiously took a few more steps toward Tom, and he moved slightly. He was real!

Finally, I stood so close to Tom that I could touch him. I thought to myself, "Why not try to touch him?" So, I did! I gently put my hand on the large feathers on his back. He remained calm, and almost seemed to like it. On the other hand, while I was calm on the outside, my heart was racing on the inside. Then, after a few minutes, I walked away slowly down the trail toward my truck. As I ran back along the river listening to water running over the rapids, I replayed the scene over and over in my mind. I rehearsed the bizarre story I would later tell my wife. I only wish I had a camera to take Tom's picture to put up on my wall!

A Lesson to Learn: *God Does Impossible Things!*

What can we learn from the story about petting Tom? I learned to believe crazy and impossible things can happen to me. If something has never been done, it doesn't mean it will never happen. God can do strange and wonderful things in our lives if we allow Him to. Don't allow your doubt to control you when you face a difficult situation. Give God a chance to work, to reveal His power, or do a miracle. He will not always give us what we want, or do the miracle we ask for, because we do not always know what's best for ourselves. If you give God a chance, He will always give you what is best and reveal His love for you, even in difficult times. And sometimes He will surprise you and do the miracle you ask for! What does this promise mean to you? Try to say it in your own words.

"God can do anything, you know—far more than you could ever imagine or guess or request in your wildest dreams! He does it not by pushing us around but by working within us, his Spirit deeply and gently within us." Ephesians 3:20-21 (The Message)

Adventure 3: A Gluttonous Trout

I cannot wait to get away from all the noisy cars and smelly trucks in my city of Atlanta. Do not misunderstand me, I love my beautiful city and the interesting people who live here. But there are six million people living close together - all trying to get to work, school, the store, or back home at the same time. After a while, the fast and crazy pace can get on your nerves, and you need a break. My friend and fishing buddy, Willie Bentley, used to describe his need to get away from "the rat race" in the big city this way. "I need to blow off the stink!" he would say at the end of a long week working as the manager of a hotel. I agreed!

I too need to blow off the stink on a regular basis. I believe that getting out in God's peaceful world is necessary for one's mental, emotional, and spiritual health.

Fishing in the Chattahoochee River north of Atlanta is one of those places of respite where the stink is easily removed. One crisp spring morning I was fishing on the bank of this river and hooked a healthy trout which put up a good fight. When I successfully landed the beautiful 14" Brown trout, I immediately noticed something strange about this fish. He had swallowed my spinner, which led to his demise, but he also had a large green frog in his throat. Now that was gluttony! Gluttony is eating more than we need, when we keep eating after we are full. The frog would fill the trout's belly for a week, but he was not satisfied. He wanted more! It was his nature to keep eating. But his gluttony got him in trouble. It was literally the death of him. The trout, instead of being the successful hunter, became the unsuccessful prey and ended up on my dinner plate. What lesson can we learn from this hungry fish?

A Lesson To Learn: *Self-control Is A Virtue*

Have you ever eaten so much food that your stomach hurt? The food was delicious, you were very hungry, and you ate too much. Maybe you ate too fast without enjoying what you ate. Here is what God say about "pigging out,"

"For the heavy drinker and the glutton will come to poverty, and drowsiness will clothe one with rags." Proverbs 23:21

Overeating will hurt us in many ways. We will not only get stomach aches, but we may get fat! We can also waste money on food and become poor. And finally, gluttony can make us lazy. We call someone like that a "couch potato," don't we?

Who wants to be a couch potato? I know you do not. Ask God to help you not make food an idol, something that you think about all the time and get overly excited about. If you get angry when you cannot eat what you want or when you want, then food has become too important. Ask God to give you self-control and to value Him and others more than you value food. He will!

Adventure 4: Get Back On The Horse

My parents sent me to Camp Pioneer in north Georgia when I was 13 years old. The camp's elevation was 2,447 feet, almost a half a mile high, which made it cold at night, even in the summer. Our family had moved from the suburbs of Washington, DC to the out-skirts of Atlanta the year before. I was too young to get a summer job and did not have many new friends, so summer camp seemed like a logical solution to fill part of my summer vacation.

The sessions at Camp Pioneer lasted an entire month! This included one entire week of whitewater canoeing down the Chattooga River, where we spent the night in tents each evening. I will never forget the trauma when several of our canoes capsized in the rapids soaking us and all our gear. I thought I might die! I am grateful we survived the river as well as the daily ration of Payday Candy Bars (made with peanuts) and PB&J sandwiches! Seared in my memory is the nausea from making and consuming sandwiches made from the premixed peanut butter and jelly in the plastic gallon jars. Even with the gourmet menu, it was still the trip of a lifetime for a teenage city boy!

We also left the main camp for one whole week of horseback riding, which also involved overnight camping. The other two weeks we spent at Camp Pioneer where we "swam" in the Icebox - an ice-cold pond that took your breath away as soon as you hit the frigid spring water. We also swam in the mountain lake, created artwork, made crafts, and played various outdoor sports. I remember making a leather belt, which I proudly wore for many years. Even though camp was a young boy's dream, there was one adventure I had with a large animal that I would rather forget.

Everything was moving along uneventfully during our trail ride until the final day. That week I gained considerable confidence working with horses which resulted in me riding one of these intimidating creatures for hours without fear. Our trail ride only involved mounting your horse, holding the reigns, and steering ever-so-slightly because the horse knew their job was to follow the other horse's rear end. I was no horse-whisperer by any stretch of the imagination, but I managed.

On the final day, however, things went awry. Just like the previous 5 days, we were mounted on our horses, following the horse in front of us along the forest trail at a slow pace. Then, the camp counselor who was leading our group got a wild idea. Since we were only a few hundred yards from the stables, why not let the horses run the rest of the way? The only problem was, we were still on top of the horses and still in the forest. We had no idea what was about to happen.

Suddenly, the horses in front of me took off at a gallop! My horse followed suit, probably knowing that fresh hay and oats were waiting in the stable. I was scared to death. I hung on for dear life! I dodged trees and limbs as my horse raced through the forest with me hanging on to the saddle for dear life. Then it happened. I was scraped off by a low-hanging branch and hit the ground hard. It hurt! Fortunately, I did not break any bones as I rolled across the ground.

Scraped, cut, bruised, and humiliated, I got up slowly and staggered back to the barn thinking, "I don't ever want to ride a horse again...ever!" Fortunately, and unfortunately as well, time seems to dull our memories of pain. My adventures with strong-willed horses picked up again when I was in college.

When I was a Freshman at Clemson University, some of my friends wanted to go ride horses one Saturday morning. One of them had a family farm not far from Clemson and they owned four horses. Somehow, they talked me into joining them. Like I said, I must have had some memory loss from my previous experience with horses four years previously.

We arrived at their farm, saddled the horses, and were about to mount them, when my friend who owned the horses said,

"All of our horses are easy to ride except that one over there," pointing to the black one near the fence. "He is a great horse but can be a little difficult to ride. So, Steve, why don't you ride him since you have experience?"

Even though my memory of the Camp Pioneer catastrophe had faded, I was reluctant to mount the horse in question. They finally talked me into it. Maybe it was pride, or maybe I wanted to overcome my fear, but I wanted to get back on a horse. We all saddled up and headed out into the pasture. I relaxed and breathed a sigh of relief thinking, "This is not too bad. Maybe it will be fun."

No problem... until my horse got out into the middle of the wide-open field. With no warning, he bolted across the field like a mad man fleeing from an angry mob. His goal was simple, get rid of the rider on his back as soon as possible! Bucking, kicking, and running full speed, it was only seconds before I was flying into the air, my heart racing, and fear totally in control. It was happening all over again! I hit the ground hard and lay there lifeless.

My friends rode over to see how I was doing. I had survived, but my ego was broken. I also questioned my friendship with the guy who put me on that crazy horse. I was angry and felt like I had been tricked.

"Why didn't he ride that wild horse? He knew he was a wild!" I thought to myself.

I had fallen off the horse and I had also "fallen in my friendship" with this guy because I felt betrayed.

Did I ever ride a horse after that? Yes, I have ridden numerous times since that adventure, but always with some lingering fear and trepidation. What lesson can be learned from falling off a horse?

A Lesson To Learn: *Get Up After A Fall*

"For a righteous man falls seven times, and rises again, But the wicked stumble in time of calamity." Proverbs 24:16

Maybe you have never ridden a horse and had a chance to be thrown off like I was – twice! Regardless, we have all fallen in one way or another in life. It could have been a literal fall, tripping while running or falling down some steps. A fall could also be failing a test in school, hurting someone with your words, or getting cut from tryouts in a play or sport. I remember being cut from my high school basketball team tryouts.

When you fall, you have a choice. Will you quit or will you get back up and try again? Will you allow failure, pain, or embarrassment to keep you on the ground, or will you ask God to help you get up, learn from your mistakes, and grow?

I was afraid of riding horses again after being thrown off, but I chose not to let my fear keep me from trying again. In the same way, many times in my life I have wanted to quit. I was afraid, embarrassed, or lacked confidence. I turned to God for strength, courage, and motivation to get up.

I encourage you to do the same when you fall. Ask God to pull you up. He is reaching out with His powerful and compassionate hand. Reach out to Him and He will help you learn from your falls.

Many times, our falls are not due to our sin, like me falling off the horse or being cut from the basketball team. On the other hand, if your fall was caused by your selfishness, then He is there to forgive you, teach you, and help you overcome. Falling is a normal part of everyone's life. What you do with it makes all the difference.

Adventure 5: Hornets Hurt

Some of us must learn the hard way. Pain can teach us lessons we will never forget, compared to learning when life is easy and fun. This story is one of those painful memories that protected me from more pain in the future.

My young friends and I headed out with their dogs to explore the evergreen forest behind our house in Asheville, North Carolina.

We bounded down the mountain behind our house to find new creatures and breathe the cool fresh air. We came to the large creek at the bottom of the mountain and began walking along the bank. On the other side was a huge, grey nest of some sort. We realized there were black insects flying in and out of the little hole in front. So, what did we do? We succumbed to the temptation and started picking up stones from the creek. We tried to see who could hit the nest which hung about 6 feet off the ground. Since the nest was the size of basketball, it did not take long before we nailed it!

We were little boys, so it did not enter our mind that these hornets could fly across the stream and find their enemy – us! They were smarter than us and much faster. I got stung a few times, but the one sting I remember was the one who bit me in the middle of my chest. I screamed in pain, grabbed my t-shirt, and ran up the hill back home. I ran in the back door with tears flowing down my cheeks.

My mother blurted out with panic in her voice,

"What happened to you? Are you alright?

Where does it hurt?"

Obviously, I was in pain, as she noticed the tears and my hand clutching my t-shirt in the middle of my chest. She was able to get me to release my hand where she discovered a dead hornet. I had squashed it and didn't let go until my mother calmed me down. Seeing the dead hornet explained everything to my mother, and she began to put some baking soda on all my stings.

A Lesson to Learn: *Pain Can Be A Great Teacher*

What good could possibly come from silly little boys throwing rocks at hornets and suffering from the painful stings? Believe it or not, pain can be a good teacher. Pain gets our attention. We usually pay better attention when we get hurt. Hurt and pain come to us in many ways - losing a game, failing a test, or a friend betraying your trust. The list is endless. We cannot escape all pain. Of course, we can bring pain on ourselves, like me and my little buddies did when we made the hornets mad.

Sometimes pain is completely out of our control. When our friends say unkind things to us, or people steal our stuff, or our parents get divorced, these are hurts we don't ask for. What can we do? Can any good come from these unwanted hurts? Yes!

Don't let the loss, defeat, failure, or pain go to waste. Let God use these difficulties to show you that His love for you never changes. Let God teach you to place your hope in Him above everything else. Then you won't be controlled by failure, pain, or other people. The hurt can make you stronger. This passage shows us how pain can grow your faith in God,

"Dear brothers and sisters, when troubles of any kind come your way, consider it an opportunity for great joy. For you know that when your faith is tested, your endurance has a chance to grow."
James 1:2-3 NLT

A Prayer When Hurting: "Thank You God for the pain in my life. Help me to forgive the people who hurt me. Thank You that you never left me or stopped loving me when it was difficult. Please use the pain to help me to hope and trust in You more than anything or anyone."

Adventure 6: Rabbit In The Garden

A rabbit had been irritating my wife and me by eating the vegetables in our garden. We were living in Clemson, South Carolina at the time and did not have much money, so the garden was an important source of food for our growing family of four.

One beautiful spring morning, my friend Rogers Kirven was driving to my house to pick me up. I was standing by the street in front of our apartment waiting for his arrival. Suddenly, the same pesky rabbit appeared across the street in the neighbor's front yard.

I think he was mocking me by just sitting there eating grass. As Rogers drove around the corner toward me, I held up my hand signaling for him to wait just a second. I said a quick prayer asking God for His help, grabbed a nearby rock, and hurled it at the rabbit. The rock hit him right in the head and he fell down dead. I could not believe it!

Rogers witnessed the bizarre event, but he did not see what I was throwing at. I ran over to the rabbit, grabbed his hind legs, and came running back to show him my trophy. His mouth fell open and his eyes popped out in disbelief. He said, "You could have knocked my eyes off with a stick!" As we drove away together, I told him the story of the pesky rabbit who would no longer have dinner in my garden! He said, "If I had not seen it, I would not have believed you!"

Have you ever read the story in the Bible about the shepherd boy, David, who fought the Philistine giant named Goliath? The giant challenged any Jewish soldier to fight him, with the winner taking the other army captive. Every day, for 40 days, Goliath came out to curse the Jews and their God. Not one Jewish soldier accepted the challenge. They all cowered in fear of the ten-foot-tall giant warrior.

David, who was just a teenager at the time of the battle, and knew nothing of warfare, volunteered to fight Goliath. When David boldly inquired about what would be done for the man who killed the giant, his three brothers, who were soldiers at the time, mocked him.

David was not deterred by their ridicule, and asked King Saul if he could go out to battle the Philistine warrior. Since no soldier had volunteered, Saul gave David his permission to represent Israel. He probably thought, "Surely this little shepherd boy will be slaughtered, and before nightfall I too will be killed, and we will all be slaves of our enemies." It was a bleak situation.

I felt the same way when I hit the rabbit. I thought, "How did I do that?" I doubted I could succeed even after asking God to help me.

A Lesson to Learn: *Attempt Difficult Goals*

There are times when you will face what seems to be an impossible situation. If it is a good and noble cause, try it! Do not allow your doubt to stop you. And, in the same way that David's brothers doubted him, your family and friends may try to persuade you not to attempt a difficult goal. Listen carefully to their arguments, make changes if necessary, but move forward if your cause is virtuous (good for others). You will not always hit the rabbit or take down a Goliath. But you will never know if you can unless you throw the rock! Ask God to help you do what you cannot do naturally - by yourself. Trust God to give you the courage to try difficult tasks. Do not be afraid to miss. Throw the rock!

How can you apply this verse to your difficulties?

"I can do everything through Christ who gives me strength."
Philippians 4:13 (New Living Bible)

Adventure 7: That Snake Won't Bite

An old photo of mules pulling a barge on the C & O Canal

It is probably hard for you to believe, but our parents would allow us to go out and play for hours if we promised to be on time

for dinner. Many times, they did not know where we were. There were no cell phones either. After dinner we could go out on our own if we returned when it got dark. We would ride our bicycles to drug store to buy candy, even though it was a mile away. No, our parents were not bad parents, the whole world was safer when I was a kid. Back then, parents did not have to worry about their children getting into trouble. All the parents in our neighborhood watched out for everyone else's children. They would not hesitate to call your parents if they saw you doing anything wrong. Neighbors were much closer when I was a kid (and not so busy.)

People walking along the C&O Canal today

We immediately stopped to get a closer look, and the snake stopped as well, coiling up into several rings. A crowd soon gathered around us staring at the big snake. I am not sure why I made this bold proclamation,

"Don't worry, I'll pick him up and move him."

I remembered hearing somewhere that the way to pick up a snake is to grab it right behind its head. (Maybe it was Chucky or Ed who told me how to pick up a snake. You'll read about these boys later in the book.)

Anyway, I courageously bent down to grab it, only to find out that the snake was faster than me. It lunged at me in self-defense, biting my outstretched hand!

"Ouch, that hurt!" I thought to myself as I pulled my hand back to my chest.

I was scared as the blood came rushing out where the fangs sunk into my hand. I felt embarrassed in front of all those strangers and my buddies, especially since I had just boldly proclaimed how easy it was to move the snake.

I ran all the way home...several miles!

What is the last thing you should do if bitten by a poisonous snake? Run! If you run, it makes the poison spread more quickly in your body. Do not run if you get bit by a snake. However, I was just a kid and did not know any better. Fortunately for me, the snake was not poisonous. As you can tell, I lived and can tell you my embarrassing snake story.

A Lesson To Learn: *Pride Comes Before A Fall*

What can we learn from my encounter with the black snake on the Canal? I learned that thinking I can do something does not mean I can. I was naïve. That means I did not know better. Some people would say I was dumb. They would be right. I thought it would be easy to pick the snake up and carry it off the towpath. The new hero with his friends. A legend in the neighborhood! Instead, the snake won, and I lost. Instead of being the hero, I was the naïve little boy who got bit. God warns us about being prideful and cocky,

"Pride goes before destruction, and a haughty spirit before stumbling."
Proverbs 16:18

Pride is when you trust yourself instead of asking God for help. It is thinking you can easily do anything by yourself, like picking up a snake, even though you have never done it or seen anyone else do it. Pride is also thinking that you are better than others. God says we stumble, or get in trouble, when we are proud. Pride leads to foolish mistakes like me trying to pick up the snake. My pride caused me to get hurt and run home to my parents...embarrassed. It was a humbling experience. That day on the canal I learned how snakes and pride are both dangerous!

If You Are Bitten By A Snake:

1. Take a picture of the snake to identify it. (is it poisonous?) Use something like the SnakeSnap app.
2. Call an ambulance immediately.
3. Do not panic and don't move.
4. Leave the snake alone.
5. Apply a pressure bandage and splint.
6. Do not wash, suck, cut or tourniquet the bite.

Adventure 8: The Fish Thief

Once again, I was trout fishing on the Chattahoochee River. On this sunny summer morning I waded out into the middle of the river through the strong current in pursuit of my quarry - the rainbow trout! That day they were elusive, and I had to work extra hard to catch them.

I finally hooked a nice fish in the cold, clear water. It fought hard to get off the spinner, but I managed to bring it within a few feet of where I was going to scoop it up with my net. The fish flailed in the water, splashing around right in front of me.

Suddenly, a large Heron swooped down and grabbed my fish in its large beak. I was shocked and yelled at the bird to let go! It kept a tight grip on my fish. It was a tug of war. Man and bird faced off in the middle of the swift water and the winner would get to eat the prized trout. After a few more angry words, and a few more jerks on my fishing rod, the Heron let go and flew off to catch his own fish. Feeling relieved and victorious, I got the fish in my net and stood there not believing what had just happened. It sounds like a real fish tale!

Lesson To Learn: *Stealing Is A Bad Idea*

It is clear what God thinks about taking something that does not belong to us.

"You shall not steal." Exodus 20:15

Stealing is taking someone's property without permission or legal right and never planning to return it. In our hearts we all know that taking something that belongs to someone else is wrong, but sometimes we do it anyway. I remember stealing some candy from the drugstore in Maryland when I was eleven years old. I did not get caught, but I felt bad afterwards. It was the same feeling of guilt that comes when you cheat on a test, take someone's toys, or steal their money.

The huge grey bird, watching me from the riverbank, wanted to steal my fish - the one that I had worked hard to catch. I know he was doing what came naturally, and he did not have a conscience like we do, but I was still angry with him.

We all have a serious problem that causes us to steal, lie, and hurt others. This problem is called sin. We cannot stop sinning without God's intervention. Just like I stopped the giant bird from stealing, God can intervene in your life and stop you from stealing, lying, or hurting others with your words or actions. Start by telling God that you have a problem and ask Him to help you stop. He promises to forgive you and change you if you admit (confess) your sins to Him,

> *"If we confess our sins, He is faithful and righteous to forgive us our sins and to cleanse us from all unrighteousness."* 1 John 1:9

Adventure 9: A Wild Boar

Blackbeard Island is an island off the coast of Georgia which harbors abundant wildlife. Blackbeard is a barrier island as well as a National Park. It is illegal to live on the island or even camp there overnight. They have so many deer and wild hogs on the island, that they have several organized hunts each year to control the population and keep the deer herd healthy. Too many deer living in one area can lead to disease and starvation. That is why they invite hunters to Blackbeard each year.

One year my friends, Dan Willis, Robert Dickinson, and I were chosen (in a lottery) to hunt on Blackbeard Island in December. We planned months ahead for this event. We practiced shooting our bows, packed our tents and all the necessary camping equipment, and got our boat and trailer ready for the expedition well in advance. You see, since no one could camp on the island, we had prepared to camp on Pine Island instead. Our plan was to get up before dawn and pack our climbing stands, bows, and lunch in the boat. Then we drove the boat several miles to Blackbeard to hunt all day. All the hunters had to leave the island when the sun went down. We were pumped about the possibilities!

Finally, the big day arrived. My buddies and I camped on the beach of Pine Island with a breathtaking view of the pounding surf and sunset. We had loaded our deer stands into our boat for the next-days hunt, so we only had to load our bows and backpacks in the dark the next morning.

We awoke two hours before sunrise on the opening day of the big hunt. We thanked God for our bowl of hot oatmeal, fruit, and juice, and we asked Him for a safe and successful hunt. Then we piled into our boat for the thirty-minute trip to Blackbeard.

I had never been there, and I had no idea where to go, so I asked God to show me a good tree to climb. I found a well-used trail with a tall Palmetto tree only 15 yards away. I started to climb the tree with my deer stand like an inchworm. I hugged the tree and pulled myself up. I had never climbed a Palmetto and was shocked to find out that their bark was covered with prickly needles. It was probably what it would be like to climb a porcupine! Fortunately, I had several layers of hunting clothes for the cold weather, so the needles did not penetrate too deeply into my skin. Once I got about 15 feet off the ground, I stopped, pulled my bow and backpack up, and put my safety belt on. I notched an arrow and could hardly wait until the sun came up. As you see in the photo, it was a beautiful sight. I could not see the ground because of the thick undergrowth except in a few openings. This made me worried because it was going to be difficult to see the deer walking by.

After a few hours, I heard a rustling in the Palmetto brush below, but could not see a thing! The animal came closer and closer. Then it passed right on by me. I felt sadness and disappointment. We had come all this way and I could not even see to shoot.

As the rustling sounds got further and further away, I decided to pray (cry out to the Lord),

"Lord, would you please bring that animal back?"

You know what happened? As soon as I said those words, I heard the animal turn and begin to come back my way!

I could tell it was going to come down a trail to my left this time. I drew my arrow back as it got closer. When the animal, as I was still not sure if it was a deer or a hog, stepped out into a small opening on the trail, I let my arrow fly. The animal took off running so fast I could not tell what it was, or if I made a good shot. It appeared not to be a deer since it was black and low to the ground, so I figured it had to be a hog. The whole scene happened so quickly that I had to rerun it over and over in my head to try and understand.

The Hunt Continued

My friend Dan came back at 11am to find me. Earlier that morning we had agreed to meet each other at a certain place on the dirt road. There is one dirt road that goes up the West side of Blackbeard Island and loops back on the Atlantic Ocean side. If a hunter shoots a deer or hog, they can drag it to the road where the game warden will pick it up in a truck. The island is five miles long, so having someone pick up your game is a fantastic idea.

When Dan saw me, he asked, "Well, how was your morning? Did you see anything?"

I blurted out, "Yes, I shot a hog, but I didn't find him!"

I had searched by myself close to where my deer stand was and only found some blood. I decided to wait for Dan to help me. I was actually a little scared because I had heard that wounded hogs can be dangerous. We returned to where I was hunting and began to follow the blood trail through thick brush. I was glad to not be alone! Then, we did not know what to do since the blood trail stopped.

We decided to stop looking and pray and ask God to find the hog for us.

We were nervous as we talked about how a wounded wild pig can be dangerous and will attack if cornered. So, we had sticks which we used to poke the bushes just in case he was alive. We figured that would give us a second or two to get a head start running. Then the adrenaline would kick in.

As I approached a large clump of undergrowth, I noticed a black tail sticking out. I poked at it and immediately felt relief as there was no movement. I glanced to the other side of the brush and saw the hog's giant head sticking out.

I yelled enthusiastically to Dan, "Dan, I found him!"

Dan ran over, gazing from one side of the bushes to the other, he exclaimed,

"I can't believe he's that big! Way to go Steve. You bagged a monster!"

A Lesson to Learn: *God Enjoys Answering Your Prayers*

It may be difficult to believe that God is concerned about you and everything in your life. The truth is, He thinks about you all the time! His thoughts about you are more than you could count!

"Many, O Lord my God, are the wonders which You have done, and Your thoughts toward us; there is none to compare with You. If I would declare and speak of them, they would be too numerous to count."
Psalm 40:5

God wants you to ask Him for things, like when I asked for the wild boar to feed my family. He promises to answer for your best. It may not always be what you think is best at the time, but it will be the best for you in the long run. So, go ahead and ask like Jesus said,

"Until now you have asked for nothing in My name; ask and you will receive, so that your joy may be made full." John 16:24

Adventure 10: Jumping On Jackets

Young boys seem to always be getting into trouble without even trying. Some would even say that little boys are not as smart as little girls. I would not go that far, but we did some remarkably dumb things that often resulted in a spanking at home. Maybe we were simply more adventurous. Here is one of those dumb things we did that really hurt and left a lasting impression!

We lived in Washington, DC at the time of this story. Every backyard was fenced in with chain link fencing. The fenced-in backyards made for great tackle football, gorilla tag, and other games with the neighborhood kids. During one such game, I was retrieving the football from the corner of our neighbor's yard, where they had a wooden box for their grass clippings. (The back-left side of our house near the fence in the photo.) For some reason, I decided to get into this box and start jumping around. It looked like so much fun, that one of my friends joined me in the box, jumping up and down next to me. Suddenly, pain shot up and down our legs. We both leapt out of the box screaming and ran straight home.

We had been stomping up and down on a yellow jacket nest! Yellow jackets are insects that live in the ground (or in your neighbor's box of grass clippings). If little boys jump on them and kill their babies (larvae), they defend themselves and sting the intruders. My friend and I were the unwelcome intruders who were stung dozens of times. Their defense plan worked, too. We ran faster than we had ever run to escape.

A Lesson To Learn: *There Are Consequences,*
Even For Our Innocent Actions

We have all done many things to hurt others, either with our words or our actions. Usually it is those closest to us that we hurt the most - our parents, our brother or sister, or our best friends. I not only fought with my brother but called him many unkind things when I was growing up. I usually got in trouble for it too, and rightfully so. It was not good for me to get away with hurting him, not to mention, he needed to be protected from his older brother.

On the other hand, there will be times where we suffer for doing the right thing. Others may misunderstand us or even be jealous of our good actions or kind words. We suffer for doing the right thing, like my friend and I jumping on the yellow jackets. We were just having fun jumping on the dead grass but got hurt for doing something innocent.

"Here is what God says about doing the right thing to help others and suffering for doing so. For what credit is there if, when you sin and are harshly treated, you endure it with patience? But if when you do what is right and suffer for it you patiently endure it; this finds favor with God."
1 Peter 2:20

Ask God to give you the strength to suffer cheerfully when you do what is right. This does not come naturally. You cannot do this alone. You need His strength to forgive others and not to retaliate when they hurt you. That is what Jesus Christ did on the cross for you. He suffered for your sins, not His, and that pleased the Father. If you follow His example, you too will please God.

Adventure 11: Stephanie
And The Snake

My daughter, Stephanie, loved going hunting with her daddy ever since she was a little girl. When she got old enough to carry a shotgun, we would put on our camouflage clothing and go turkey hunting together. As you heard in the story, "Petting Tom," wild turkeys have excellent eyesight and they can run faster than us. They can also fly to the top of big trees to get away from danger.

One cool spring morning Stephanie and I went turkey hunting. She is now married and has four young children, but we still find the time to hunt together. We had recently seen some turkeys in the area, so we were optimistic about our chances. We both went into the forest, just off the edge of a large field, and sat down against a tree to hunt. We sat about 20 feet apart so that she could look in one direction while I looked the other direction, giving us a better opportunity to spot the turkeys. I made a few calls imitating a hen.

Suddenly, Stephanie jumped up and screamed!

She scared me and I jumped up yelling, "What's the matter?"

Stunned, she said, "There is a huge black snake trying to get me! He was slithering along over there and then started coming straight at me! He was quickly getting closer and closer. I jumped up before he ran into me."

After a few minutes we were able to calm down, and then we both laughed with relief as we recounted the story. The snake was not trying to attack her. It was probably as scared of Stephanie as she was of it - and happy that we left.

A Lesson To Learn: *God Is With Us When We Are Scared*

Have you ever seen a snake in its natural environment? Were you afraid like Stephanie? Maybe you jumped and screamed.

Sometimes scary things can turn out to be harmless like Stephanie's non-poisonous black snake.

There are other times when the scary things *can harm you*. Whenever you are afraid, God tells you to remember that He is with you and He will take care of you. Just like the mother bird in this drawing takes care of her young during the storm, so God will protect you.

Thank God for His promises,

'Do not fear, for I am with you.
Do not anxiously look about you, for I am your God.
I will strengthen you, surely, I will help you,
Surely I will uphold you with My righteous right hand.'
Isaiah 41:10

Here is the same verse in two different translations.

Don't panic. I'm with you.
There's no need to fear for I'm your God.
I'll give you strength. I'll help you.
I'll hold you steady, keep a firm grip on you.
(The Message)

Don't be afraid, for I am with you.
Don't be discouraged, for I am your God.
I will strengthen you and help you.
I will hold you up with my victorious right hand.
(New Living Translation)

Adventure 12: Where's My Contact Lens?

A light rain started falling one afternoon while we were hunting deer in Maxey's, Georgia. My old friend, David Greenwood, and I were hunting on his family property. When the sun went down, we got down from our tree stands and went to meet each other and walk back to the truck.

David came over to where I was hunting and found me wandering around in the dark forest looking on the ground. I had rubbed my eyes with the back of my hand to get some rain off my face. I accidentally touched my eye and knocked my contact out. I had been looking for it for ten minutes when David arrived on the scene. By then it was so dark I could only see his flashlight.

He saw me staring at the wet ground and said, "What's wrong? What are you looking for?" I said sadly, "I lost my contact and can't find it. I have been looking for it for the last ten minutes. The rain makes everything shine like a contact lens. I don't think I'll ever find it!"

Everywhere I looked on the wet leaves looked like contact lenses! I was upset and discouraged. David could tell by the sound of my voice that I was upset. He walked over and put his arm on my shoulder and said, "God knows where your contact lens is. Let us pray and ask Him to show us." I knew he was right, but I still doubted that God was going to show us where a tiny, clear, contact lens was in a dark forest where all the leaves were glistening from the rain. I bowed my head anyway and David prayed. "God, thank you that you know everything. Please show us where Steve's contact lens is if it is Your will for us to find it. Thank you. In Jesus' name. Amen." You will be surprised to find out what happened next.

I opened my eyes while my head was still bowed down after praying. What was that on the end of my wet boot? It was my contact lens! It had been there all along. It never fell off my boot, even though I walked all around the forest in the wet leaves looking for it. Crazy, eh? We both rejoiced and thanked God for answering our prayers!

A Lesson to Learn: *God Knows Everything!*

God knew where my contact was all the time. Isn't that amazing? He waited until we stopped and asked Him for help before He showed me where it was. What are some things that are missing in your life that you want to find? Have you stopped and asked God to show you where they are or to give them to you? He cares about you and everything that is important to you, even a little contact lens!

"Nothing in all creation is hidden from God's sight. Everything is uncovered and laid bare before the eyes of him to whom we must give account." Hebrews 4:13

Adventure 13: The One That Got Away

"What had happened?" I wondered to myself. The deer jumped up in the air and then bolted off when I released my arrow. He ran away so quickly I was not sure what I had seen.

"Had I made a bad shot?" I thought long and hard trying to understand.

I finally surmised that my arrow shaved the white hair off the big buck's ribs and lodged in his back leg. He broke the arrow and ran off, not mortally wounded, but to heal and continue his long life. I felt sick in my stomach as I admitted to myself that the trophy buck got away. It was hard not to feel discouraged.

What did I learn from this heart-breaking disappointment? Instead of being depressed for a long time, I took comfort in knowing that I had successfully found this trophy buck's habitat. I was able to remain undetected by the willy deer and get off a shot as well. Many hunters were not blessed with such an opportunity. God also gave me the skill to hit my target, even if it was not the best shot.

I also learned that it is never a failure to try something difficult. I gained confidence. I learned that to live with disappointment takes faith in God and His promises. I did not give up and quit hunting after that disappointing hunt, but I enjoy the sport more than ever! I have harvested many deer since then, including some large bucks. I am still waiting for a trophy like the one that got away.

A Lesson to Learn: *Good Can Come From Losing*

We play to win the soccer match, the chess game, or the science fair. None of us like to lose. Have you noticed how much easier it is to win the game, to bring home the big buck, or make a perfect grade on a test, than it is to be unsuccessful? On the other hand, being unsuccessful can be a powerful teacher - if we respond well. We can learn valuable lessons from the hard times, failures, and setbacks.

It hurts to lose. If you do not look for the good that can come from losing, you will suffer in vain. But, if you welcome the failure, you can grow in character. If you will embrace the pain and try to understand God's purpose, you will mature, as these verses promise,

"And not only this, but we also exult in our tribulations, knowing that tribulation brings about perseverance; and perseverance, proven character; and proven character, hope; and hope does not disappoint, because the love of God has been poured out within our hearts through the Holy Spirit who was given to us." Romans 5:3-5

When you fail to accomplish your goal you need to ask, "Did God's love for me change?" Of course not! You may ask, "Then why do I feel so bad?" Watch out for those tricky feelings! Your feelings can fool you and cause you to doubt God's goodness and love. God's love has nothing to do with our circumstances, winning or losing, success or failure. We can know He loves us all the time because He gave us His Son Jesus to die for our sins. That love never changes for you!

"We can rejoice, too, when we run into problems and trials, for we know that they help us develop endurance. And endurance develops strength of character, and character strengthens our confident hope of salvation. And this hope will not lead to disappointment. For we know how dearly God loves us, because he has given us the Holy Spirit to fill our hearts with his love." NLT

Adventure 14: A Surprise For Mom And Dad

Every kid loves summer camp. Summer camp always provided me with new adventures and fun no matter how old I was. I was 11 years old when my parents sent me to camp in Pennsylvania for a week of swimming, hiking, archery, overnight camping, and arts and crafts. I saw, smelled, heard, and touched God's creation with a bunch of other kids from Washington, DC my age. We encountered new creatures in their environments and expanded our knowledge of life. Here are some of our experiences.

We did many things I had never done before, like camping, finding our own food, and looking for treasures. I remember camping overnight in tents on a large river somewhere in the Pennsylvania countryside. The river was wide and impressive - it looked more like a lake. Next to our campsite was a large, inviting field of corn. A few of us could not resist the temptation to run into the corn maze. We slipped away from our counselor and took some of the ripe golden corn from the cornfield. We ate it back at our campsite. I do not remember why we consumed the contraband, because I know they fed us. Maybe we got tired of the 'gourmet' camp food (Ha! Gourmet peanut butter & jelly sandwiches or Spam/Vienna Sausages from a can), or we were simply curious. Whatever the reason, uncooked corn did not taste too bad to a hungry kid.

When we were hiking back to the bus that would drive us back to the camp, I noticed something strange not far off the trail. It was a pile of white bones from some large animal. Immediately I shot off the path and grabbed the largest bone I could find. The other guys followed and collected their own white bones. It was like I had just found a treasure chest on a deserted island. All my buddies wanted to hold mine since it was the largest. They passed it around with eyes wide open. None of us had ever seen anything so cool. Our counselor told us that it was the huge skull of a cow!

Of course, I had to take my new-found treasure home to show it off to my parents. And that is what I did, lugging it along with my suitcase stuffed with smelly clothes and the beaded necklace and potholders I had made in arts and crafts.

The camp bus pulled into our school parking lot filled with anxious parents waiting to collect their kids. The kids bounded off the bus, talking and screaming at the same time, anxious to tell their parents how much fun they had shooting bows and arrows, swimming in the lake, and riding horses for the first time.

Me, I had the mother of all treasures in my arms as I stepped down the stairs of the bus. When my mom and dad saw me carrying the giant cow skull, you can imagine the shock and wonder on their faces. They quickly tried to gather their thoughts to say something positive to their son.

"What is that?" They blurted out as soon as they saw the large sun-bleached cow skull.

"Where did you find that skull?" Answering their own question.

"Where did you get it?"

All their questions poured out of their mouths at once before I could answer the first one.

When we got in the car, I started from the beginning and told them how I found the cow skull while we were camping overnight in tents. I hardly took a breath as I recounted slipping off into the cornfield, eating raw corn, and how we didn't sleep very much that night as we listened to the waves lapping the shoreline along the river and talked into the early morning hours. I had great parents! They were supportive and let me keep the skull on my dresser where it became an object of awe to all my neighborhood buddies who came to see this phenomenon. After all, what other kid did they know who had a real cow skull?

A Lesson to Learn: *What Is A Real Treasure?*

"Do not store up for yourselves treasures on earth, where moth and rust destroy, and where thieves break in and steal. But store up for yourselves treasures in heaven, where neither moth nor rust destroys, and where thieves do not break in or steal; for where your treasure is, there your heart will be also." Matthew 6:19-21

The cow skull was a treasure to me as a little boy. I do not know what happened to it. Maybe I got tired of it or my mother did and tossed it in the trash. I had a coin collection that my father helped me start as a young boy. Some of the coins were rare, silver dollars, silver quarters, Buffalo Head nickels, and Indian Head pennies. The collection was especially valuable to me because the hours my dad and I had spent together was priceless. When I got married, I kept my coin collection in our apartment. My wife and I met a homeless woman and invited her to stay with us. We wanted to show her God's love and tell her how she could have a relationship with Him. The next day she disappeared along with one of my wife's best sweaters and my entire coin collection. In the verse above, Jesus said it is possible for, "thieves break in and steal" our treasures on earth.

Maybe someone stole something of yours that was valuable. How did Jesus say we should invest our lives?

People treasure everything imaginable. Most of the things people collect are temporary, like my prized cow skull and rare coin collection, and will not last forever. What lasts forever? People. People are the only things that last forever. Only people are eternal. Of course, everyone's body will eventually die and be buried. But our soul is eternal and will live forever with God or separated from Him.

God treasures **you** and longs for a relationship with you. How you respond to His love and offer of this relationship is completely up to you. If you chose Jesus Christ as your Lord and Savior, God promises that you *have* eternal life!

"Truly, truly, I say to you, he who hears My word, and believes Him who sent Me, has eternal life, and does not come into judgment, but has passed out of death into life." John 5:24

After you believe in Jesus and ask Him to forgive your sins and make you His child, you can then store up treasures in heaven. The Holy Spirit comes to live in you the moment you believe in Christ, and He gives you the power to treasure Him and others. That is "laying up treasure in heaven." How exciting! How rewarding!

A prayer to pray: *"Dear God, thank You for making me Your child when I believed in Jesus. Now, I want to treasure others as never before, and in a way that honors You. Help me live my life for You and for others and not for myself."*

Adventure 15: Washing Toads

My grandparents lived in the small farming town of Fountain, North Carolina. My Granddad was a rural mail carrier and a farmer who grew corn, soybeans, and tobacco. He also loved to hunt quail, or, as he called them, partridges. Quail are small game birds that live in the forests and along the edges of corn and soybean fields where they came to eat. My passion for hunting was born in the fields and forests of Pitt County, North Carolina because of my grandfather's enthusiasm for quail hunting and the great outdoors.

Fountain was a small country town where the farmers produced the corn and soybeans for big processing plants. The locals also bought their groceries and farming supplies from several stores, including Yelverton's, R. J. Fountain's, and Jefferson's General Store. They only purchased items they could not make themselves back at the farm. They would come to town to get Dr. Beasley to fill a prescription from Beasley's Drug store. There was only one gas station, the Esso, which was located on the corner of Main Street and Highway 258. Back then all gas stations were full-service stations. That meant several men came out at one time to wash your windows, open your hood to check your oil level, check your tire pressure, and pump your gas, all for free. There were no self-serve gas stations until many years later. The train came through twice a day collecting agricultural products my grandfather and the other farmers brought into town.

Life in the small town of Fountain, population of less than 500, was drastically different than our life in the suburbs of Washington, DC. So was the culture! Our granddad drove slowly. Everyone talked slowly. The food was different from our mother's meatloaf, tuna casserole, and chipped beef on toast. Grandmother was an artist in the kitchen! She prepared delicious meals with plenty of home-grown vegetables, and she always served tasty desserts like apple pie, red velvet cake, and strawberry pie made from their own strawberries. I remember one summer I went to work on their farm. We got up early on a Saturday morning and drove (very slowly) to the North Carolina coast where we picked gallons of blueberries. I had fun picking the fat, juicy, dark-blue berries, while eating as many as I could in the process. We took our haul of berries back to Fountain where Grandmother froze most of them. That night she made a fresh blueberry pie for dessert, covered in vanilla ice cream. Those memories are forever imprinted on that little boy's mind and heart. In my opinion, Grandmother may have been the best cook on the planet. No offense to my mother or my wife, of course. Life in the country was simply different. A good different.

They also spoke a "foreign language" in Fountain that took some time for us to learn. The southern drawl was slow, like the entire lifestyle of country living. "Over yonder" meant something over there. And, when someone said they were, "fixing to go to the store" or "fixing to do the wash" it meant they were getting ready to do something. They also said, "Y'all come here. Or, "Did Y'all see that?"

It took us some time for us kids to understand that the translation for Y'all was *you all.*

Even though my mother had been raised on a farm in North Carolina, she graduated from the University of North Carolina where she met my father, Don Nelson, from New York City.

Since I attended school in Washington, DC, it took me some time to catch on to Fountain's southern brand of English. My brother and I were unkind and made fun of these different people and laughed at the way they did things. We were young, insecure, and mean to Chucky and Ed. Not one of my finest hours.

My mother was my grandparent's only daughter. She had two brothers, my Uncle Dave and Uncle Howard. Uncle Howard had two sons, Robbie and Jamie, who would often be in Fountain at the same time as us, usually on a holiday. After endless hours of playing Chinese checkers and card games on the back porch, the four of us would go out exploring the town. Since this story is about frogs and toads, I need to make sure you know something about them first.

Frog above and Toad below

Frog and Toad

Toads and frogs are similar, but there are some important differences. Look at the photographs of the frog and toad above. Frogs live near water and have smooth, wet skin that makes them look slimy. Whereas toads do not need to live near water, and they have dry, bumpy skin. Frogs have longer hind legs which makes them able to jump higher than toads. Toads have a fatter body, and nothing likes to eat them for dinner, unlike frogs which have many predators that consider them a delicacy. Even people eat frogs! I remember my uncle Dave took me out for dinner when I was a teenager and they served frog legs. They tasted like chicken, and I enjoyed them. There were no toad legs on the buffet that day!

Toad Capital Of The World

I am not sure why, but Fountain must have been the toad capital of the world. You have never seen so many of these little hoppity creatures in your life. They were nocturnal, which means they only came out at night to eat bugs, usually around the streetlights. The streetlights attracted insects which in turn attracted the hordes of toads. My brother Kurt and I, along with our cousins, Robbie and Jamie, were entertained by these fat little toads. We would chase them and scare them off the streets. Toads are slow, remember, as they have short legs, so we had to be careful not to step on them. In the morning, we would find dozens of dead slow-moving toads that had been squashed by cars during the night. It was gross!

Chuck, who was known to us kids as Chucky, was a young boy who lived in Fountain only a few blocks away from my grandparents. Ed was one of Chucky's good friends, so we always saw the pair of them together. They provided some excitement for us with their unexpected behavior. After all, little city boys run out of things to do in Fountain in 24 hours. The following is one such incident...

One day Kurt and I, along with Robbie and Jamie, were walking down the street near our grandparent's house. When we passed by Chucky's house, he spotted us and came running out of the back yard all excited about something. Of course, Ed was not far behind him.

Chucky said, "I got me a washing machine over yonder" pointing to his backyard.

"I'm washing toads. Y'all wanta come see 'em?"

How could any kid refuse such an offer? Our curiosity was killing us. We were compelled to go see this strange event. After all, nobody washed toads in Washington, DC!

The four of us all squeezed around the old washer and peered down into the rusty tub. There were six to eight big brown toads swimming for their lives. Who knows what those poor toads thought after being captured and tossed in the water where they were spun around and around! Remember, toads are not fond of water. It was a spectacle we never forgot. It was entertaining. We laughed about that bizarre event with our cousins every time we saw them at Thanksgiving reunions.

Chucky's old washing machine and the new model

I was not aware at the time, but God was doing something in my heart through my encounter with Chuck and Ed washing the toads. He was showing me I had a problem that only He could help me with. It was ten years later that I learned the following important lesson.

A Lesson To Learn: *God Loves Everyone Equally*

This verse tells us who God thinks is valuable.

"I now truly understand that God does not show favoritism in dealing with people, but in every nation the person who fears (respects) Him and does what is right is welcomed before Him." Acts 13:34-35 NET

God invites everyone into a personal relationship with Himself. He cares about people of every color, in every culture, regardless of how much education or wealth they have.

When I was a young boy, I looked down on Chuck and Ed because they sounded less educated and lived in a small farm town. I was unkind the way I spoke to them and my brother and I made fun of them. I thought I was a better person.

The good news is that God can change sinful people like me. God showed me that He loves everyone equally. He does not have favorites. He is not prejudiced like I was toward Chuck and Ed.

When I was nineteen, I asked God to forgive me for being unkind to others, including Ed and Chuck, my brother, and my parents. He did. I asked Jesus Christ to take control of my life and make me a new person who would treat others with respect. He did! I'm grateful that God forgives us when we are truly sorry.

Is there anyone you have looked down on, said unkind things to, or had a bad attitude toward like I did with Chuck and Ed? If so, ask God to forgive you and change you into someone who does not show favoritism.

If you have never asked God to make you His child, then why not do that right now? God says,

"Whoever will call on the name of the Lord will be saved." Romans 10:13

You can say this to God, *"Thank You God that Jesus died on the cross for my sins and rose from the dead to give me new life. I trust what Jesus did for me to make me your child. I am not trusting my good deeds to make me clean. I ask You to forgive all my sins and to make me a new person. I want to be your child. I give my life to You. Thank You for answering my prayer."*

Adventure 16: 30,000 Stingers!

I got a call from the manager of Publix Grocery in east Atlanta that went like this: "Hello, is this Steve Nelson the beekeeper? I'm the manager of Publix on Briarcliff Road. We have a massive swarm of honeybees in our parking lot. Our customers are upset. Can you come right now and remove them for us? We don't want to kill them."

This immediately piqued my interest. I was a new beekeeper who wanted to have his own bees but did not have a clue how to rescue a swarm. Sure, I had attended our club's one day course for beginner beekeepers, but I was totally inexperienced. I did not have any beehives at my house at that point. It would be my first honeybee swarm. I felt nervous and afraid as I thought about collecting 30,000 bees with 30,000 stingers. Was I crazy?

I pretended to be confident and responded to the manager, "Yes, I will be there in 25 minutes!"

I quickly threw my bee suit and an empty hive into my truck, and off I went, unsure of what might happen when I arrived. But before

I left the house, I called Jerry Wallace, my new friend and beekeeping mentor.

"Hi Jerry, this is Steve. There is a swarm at the Publix Grocery Store not far from your house and I am going to go get it. Would you be able to come help me?" (Please, please, please!)

Jerry graciously replied, "Hey Steve. I would be happy to meet you over there. Do you have everything you'll need?'

"Yes, I think so." I said as I proceeded to list everything I had packed in my truck.

"I'll see you there. Thank you very much Jerry!" I said with a tremendous sigh of relief.

When I arrived, the entire area had been taped off with yellow tape, making it look like a crime scene. A huge mass of bees had collected under one of the little metal roofs where customers left their empty grocery carts. Of course, nobody dared go anywhere near the hundreds of bees flying around this structure.

The two store managers were there to meet me. They explained how the pest control company would not kill honeybees. That is when they decided to call a local beekeeper to come rescue the bees. I did not want to let them know that I was a novice beekeeper, stalling for his mentor to show up for fear these men would freak out. As we were chatting, their eyes popped out and their mouths dropped open. I turned around to find out what they were staring at. It was Jerry with his hand on 30,000 bees with 30,000 stingers!

I thought to myself, "Is he insane? What in the world is he doing?"

I went over to "help" Jerry with the bees. He would take a frame from my hive and hold it up to the swarm. The bees smelled the wax on the frames and began to crawl onto it. When the frame was covered with bees, Jerry would place it into the hive box. He did that with all 10 frames until most of the bees were inside.

Honeybees communicate by smell (pheromones). They smell the queen's pheromone and follow her. The worker bees also emit a pheromone to let the other workers outside the hive know that she has moved into a new location. That is how they "talk" to one another. Is not God amazing!

Jerry used the smoker to move the several thousand remaining bees off the metal beam. A smoker is a small device in which the beekeeper burns something to make smoke to blow on the bees. The smoke calms the bees because it inhibits the bee's pheromones from working. Bees send out pheromones to tell the other bees to defend the hive, or in this case, sting those guys! This tactic got the remaining bees to leave the metal beam and start flying around. Then they smelled the queen in my hive box below them on the ground and gradually relocated to their new home. We waited an hour or so and then closed the box. I took the 30,000 bees to my apiary in our backyard. I will never forget the rush of adrenaline from that adventure!

A Lesson to Learn: *Everyone Needs A Good Friend*

Jesus taught us that laying down our own life for our friends is the greatest expression of love.

"Greater love has no one than this, that one lay down his life for his friends." John 15:13

My good friend, Jerry, "laid down his life" for me that day when he stopped what he was doing to come help me rescue my first swarm of honeybees.

Jerry not only came and helped me get the bees in my hive, but he patiently answered my questions and explained what he did in detail. Because Jerry made the time to teach me, the next time I got a swarm call, I was able to do it all by myself.

Do you have good friends like Jerry? If not, ask God to give you some. More importantly, ask Him to help you to be a friend to others. Ask Him to help you lay down your life as Jesus did for you on the cross. He gave everything up for you. If you asked Jesus to be your Savior, then He now calls you His friend!

"I have called you friends, because I have revealed to you everything I heard from my Father." John 15:15

Adventure 17: 103 Fish

I learned how to fish from my granddad. More importantly, I learned how to live from that wise old man. Even though Floyd Davis Turnage was a stern man of few words, he taught me many valuable life lessons, mostly by how he lived. He was known in his community for being a man of integrity and kindness. Grandad taught me by his example how to work hard without complaining when we worked side by side in the hot tobacco fields when I was a teenager. He taught me to notice and appreciate God's amazing creation when he showed me the circle in the dirt where the quail had gathered the night before to sleep. He taught me not to waste an animal's life by shooting only what would ensure a healthy population for next season. And, he explained why we only kept enough fish to feed us or to give away to needy families he knew. My granddad was an original conservationist. He respected God and all of God's creatures, and he taught me to do the same. Those were valuable life-lessons that did not come from a book or classroom.

Learning to fish with my granddad was much more than simply catching fish. The experience started with collecting bait - digging for earthworms by the pig pen. The lesson I learned - the harder you must work for something (in this case it was a fish), the more valuable it becomes. You appreciate it more than if someone gave it to you. Digging for worms was hard work, but exciting for a young boy from the city.

Uncle Hardy raised cows on his farm outside of Fountain, North Carolina. He dug a pond the size of a football field for his cows to have easy access to water. That is where I learned to love fishing. Grandad demonstrated how to bait the hook with a wiggling earthworm and how to swing the line out over the water, dropping the hook and small weight into the water where he wanted it. He instructed me on how to watch the cork bob up and down when a fish started nibbling at the bait, to keep the line tight, but not to pull on it until the cork went under the water. The first time he yanked on the line and pulled up a fat bluegill, I was hooked!

Granddad left me at the pond to go do some work around his farm, across the road, and he returned several hours later. I started catching bluegills (also called bream) and small bass, throwing most of them back in because they were too small. The cows watched curiously when they came to drink nearby. God revealed Himself to me that day through the fish, the cows, the Carolina blue sky, and the Red-winged Blackbirds making their nests in the reeds along the bank. The blackbirds were not fond of me invading their space and would dive bomb my head, squawking loudly if I got too close to their young hidden in the nests. I drank deeply of God's creation, unaware of the impact it had on my soul. I also learned that I would be okay being alone. Learning to do things on my own. I learned by doing, not just reading about it in Outdoor Life magazine.

Ownership came from getting out there in God's creation. I became a fisherman for life. I now had experience fishing. Experience! I had gone beyond theory to living it out. I could say with confidence, "I know how to fish because I've done it." I had been successful, and I had suffered disappointment whenever a fish wiggled off my hook and fell back into the pond. One big bass even broke my pole and got away. I wanted my granddad to be proud of me, and that is why I counted the fish I caught that day. I managed to land 103 fish in one day! I was so lost in God's creation that I never worried about being alone for hours. When it was time to go home, it was too soon!

A Lesson to Learn: *We Learn Best By Doing*

My grandfather showed me how to catch fish and then he wisely left me there at Uncle Hardy's pond to learn to fish on my own. That is how we all learn best, by practice, by trial and error. We must try to do something, make mistakes, and figure things out. We should ask our parents or trusted friends for advice along the way, and watch them in action, but we must get out there and fish on our own to be a real fisherman.

In the same way, God wants you to own your faith in Him. Your parents and friends can show you how to pray, read the Bible, and trust God in all things. But it must be your choice to follow Jesus and to obey Him. You cannot rely on their faith to carry you through life. You must learn to trust God and obey His word yourself as these verses tell us...

"Don't just listen to God's word. You must do what it says. Otherwise, you are only fooling yourselves. For if you listen to the word and do not obey, it is like glancing at your face in a mirror. You see yourself, walk away, and forget what you look like. But if you look carefully into the perfect law that sets you free, and if you do what it says and don't forget what you heard, then God will bless you for doing it." James 1:22-25

Ask God to give you the desire and strength get to know Jesus Christ better by reading His word and practicing it.

Adventure 18: A Hardheaded Owl

Early one cold December morning, I was driving in my truck to go deer hunting in the Oconee National Forest. It was a pitch-black, moonless night as I passed through an area with large pine trees crowding in on both sides of the road. I felt like I was driving in a dark tunnel. It was so monotonous that it was putting me to sleep.

Bam! Suddenly, I was jerked back to full consciousness by a loud bang against the side of my truck.

"Did someone just throw a rock at me?" was my immediate reaction.

I hit my brakes, coming to a quick stop, and got out to survey the side of my truck with my flashlight. I did not see any damage. The rock theory made no sense because there were no houses anywhere to be seen along this isolated stretch of road.

I got back in my truck and turned around. I returned to where I thought the incident had occurred and searched for what may have hit me. I found a small owl laying on the pine straw. He was ridiculously small - maybe 8 inches tall. He was laying on the ground dead, or so I thought.

I felt bad for the little bird and thought I should not leave him there, so I picked him up and carefully laid him in the bed of my truck against the cab. I drove to my hunting site, parked my truck, and got all my gear and went hunting all morning - with no luck.

When I returned, I peered into the truck bed. I was shocked to see the little owl was standing up! He was alive!

Since he had not flown away, I concluded that he must have been seriously injured. What should I do? I thought, if I left him there, he would probably die. Then I had a crazy idea. I put him in the truck next to me on the passenger side floor and drove an hour and a half back home. He stood there on the floor mat the entire trip wobbling back and forth – most likely from the shock. Or maybe because he had never ridden in a truck before.

As I drove home, I contemplated what to do. Should I take him home and attempt to nurse him back to health, like the baby rabbits we tried to save as a child, or should I take him to our local vet. I concluded that the vet would be his best chance of survival, so I dropped him off after telling them my bizarre story. They were happy to take him in and thanked me.

I checked on my little Eastern Screech Owl every few weeks. The good news is, he had a full recovery and was released back into the wild to hunt again. I hope he did not try to attack any more trucks and lived a long and happy life! What can we learn from the little owl who once appeared dead and came back to life?

A Lesson To Learn: *Life After Death Is Possible*

I sincerely believed that the little owl was dead. It seemed impossible to me when I picked up his lifeless body that he could come back to life. I was shocked to see him standing up in the bed of my truck looking at me with his big yellow eyes. Obviously, he was not dead, only unconscious. Dead animals do not come back to life.

Dead people do not come back to life either, unless....

Jesus Christ was crucified by Roman soldiers and hung on a wooden cross where He died. When He miraculously rose from the grave after three days, it demonstrated the power of God! God was telling the world that Jesus was the only one worthy to pay for all the sins of every person, and to offer each of us new life here and now, and life with Him eternally. Wow! Read this amazing promise...

Jesus said to her, "I am the resurrection and the life; he who believes in Me will live even if he dies, and everyone who lives and believes in Me will never die. Do you believe this?" John 11:25-26

Do you believe that Jesus is the resurrection and the life? Have you asked Him to forgive your sins and be your Savior and Lord? That is what it means to believe in Him. This is also called the second birth, the spiritual birth, that Jesus Christ offers you. If you have done this, then you too will never die. Your body will die, but your soul will live on eternally with your Creator and Savior! That is good news!

Interesting Facts: The Eastern Screech Owl's eyes and beak are yellow. Their feet are large for their size, and they have feathers on their toes. The tufts on their head that look like large ears are just feathers. Their ears are on the side of their head. Like most owls, they can fly silently because God gave them large wings and serrated feathers that muffle the sound of the air flowing over their wings. This design makes it possible for them to sneak up on their prey undetected.

Adventure 19: What Is In That Hole?

Linda Lamb was one of my neighbors in Raleigh, North Carolina. I was 5 years old when I first met this energetic, blond-haired little girl.

I learned many things from Linda but learning how to catch Tiger Beetle larva is at the top of my list. Linda showed me something that I had never seen and did not know existed. There were little larva living in small holes in ground, out of sight and out of mind to most people. She explained how we could catch one of these ugly lava by putting a long stem of grass into the deep hole, waiting until it bit the other end, and then quickly jerking it out of the hole. I was fascinated by the idea!

Picking up a suitable stem of grass, Linda carefully inserted it into the little hole. Then she placed her thumb and index finger on either side of the stem, right above the ground, waiting and watched intently. As soon as the long stem moved, she snatched it up in one swift motion. A scary larva with big pincers came flying out of the hole and landed on the ground! To me, this was magical.

LARVA

Bristly knobs
to hold larva
in tunnel

Wide, flat
head with
widely
spaced
jaws

Circular, deep
tunnel with
funnel-shaped
top

Geoff Balme
NC STATE UNIVERSITY

Teaching someone to do something means that you care enough to take the time and make the effort necessary for them to be able to do what you can do. Linda was that kind of teacher for me. It took me a while to be able to get the stem down far enough and learn when to pull it out. Eventually I became a professional and have taught all 7 of my children and most of our 20 grandchildren this fine art. If you have never done it, go try it! It is fun. Then teach it to your friends, your children, or your grandchildren.

A Lesson To Learn: *Good Friends Teach You Good Things ------*
Especially About God

Jesus said to His friends, *"No longer do I call you slaves, for the slave does not know what his master is doing; but I have called you friends, for all things that I have heard from My Father I have made known to you."* **John 15:15**

Jesus taught His friends everything about God. He wanted them to know His Father in a personal way and how much He loved them. He did not keep any secrets from them but told them all the important things about how to live a happy life with God. He taught them how to love God and how to love people, even people who were mean to them. He taught them how to "fish for men" by telling them who God was and how they could know Him personally. *"Follow Me, and I will make you fishers of men."* (Matthew 4:19) They learned and became great fishers of men, bringing many unbelievers to faith in Jesus.

A real friend cares enough to take the time to teach you important life lessons. Linda was a real friend who patiently taught me how to catch the little Tiger Beetle larva living underground in our backyard. We had hours of fun exploring God's creation together.

In the same way today, friends teach their friends how to do things. Bad friends will teach you things that hurt you, get you in trouble with your parents, and maybe even the police. They may teach you how to make fun of others, disrespect your parents and teachers, lie, or steal. Stay away from those kinds of people.

Good friends will teach you how to do good things - the right thing in the eyes of God. They will teach you how to be kind to everyone, respect those in authority, and to forgive instead of getting angry and fighting. Find those kinds of friends and learn from them. They are valuable!

Adventure 20: Captured By Butterflies

My family lived in the nation's capital when I was in 5th grade. I do not remember how I became interested in this hobby, but I began regularly going outside to catch butterflies in our neighborhood. I was so fascinated by these beautiful little creatures that I eventually started my own butterfly collection and displayed it on our wall.

I would run through our neighborhood in Bethesda, Maryland, going from yard to yard, searching for butterflies. As is often the case with a hobby, the hobbyist ends up being captured by what they collect. I was captivated by the varieties of colorful butterflies that I saw. I would dream of new places to find them, and what to do with them afterwards.

Catching a butterfly was not an easy mission. It involved locating the flowers where they could be found - then, patiently sneaking up on them as they flitted from flower to flower drinking nectar.

I had to be very patient and get close enough to reach the butterfly without alarming them. If they caught even the slightest movement, they would swiftly fly away to safety. Once I was in position, I would quickly swoop my large butterfly net sideways to snatch them off the flower and quickly pull the net to the ground. If I went straight down on top of the butterfly, I not only caught the insect, but the entire plant. That never worked because it could smash my prize catch or allow room for the butterfly to escape. Catching the butterfly without damaging it was an art form that took some time to perfect, not unlike setting a hook in a fish takes time to learn as well. It was a challenging game that I never tired of playing.

After catching a butterfly in my large net, I immediately put it in a jar containing formaldehyde, a chemical preservative. The butterfly died instantly, protecting its delicate wings.

Mounting butterflies to exhibit involved removing them from the jar while they were still flexible, and carefully pinning them to cardboard. They would be stiff after a few days on the cardboard and could be transferred to a shadow box frame. The shadow box was deep enough to pin a butterfly in its natural flying position. They looked like they were still alive when I finished. My butterflies hung on the wall in our house for years and caught the attention of many. Capturing and collecting butterflies made me a proud young boy. It captured my little heart every time.

A Lesson To Learn: *God Wants to Capture Your Heart*

"Give me your heart, my son, and let your eyes delight in my ways."
Proverbs 23:26

In the same way that I was captured by the radiant colors, graceful flight, and delicacy of the butterflies, God wants to capture your heart with Himself! He wants you to be enamored with Him – His beauty, His power, His love, and His plan for your life. He created you, and He wants you for Himself, not because He is selfish, but because He is good. We are His prize possession – not to be harmed as the butterflies that I captured, but to be set free from sin through faith in His Son Jesus and become His child. Jesus said, "I came that they may have life and have it abundantly." John 10:10 Why not allow God to capture you and give you abundant life? Pray this prayer to Him now.

A Prayer to Pray: "God, You are amazing! You made this incredible world with all the beautiful creatures, including the butterflies. You did it all because you love us! Therefore, I surrender my entire life to you, all my possessions, by family, friends, plans, and desires. I give you total control. Capture my heart with Yourself! Thank You that I am Your child and will be with You forever! Thank you that I am so valuable to you that you sent Your only Son, Jesus Christ, to capture me for Yourself!"

Adventure 21: Burning Down The Woods

Little boys and matches are a dangerous combination. We have all heard our parents warn us,

"Don't play with fire. You will get burned."

Obviously, I must have had a hearing problem as a kid because...

One fall day a few of my buddies and I went out exploring in the woods near my house in Washington. We were three innocent 11-year-old boys out looking for turtles in the forest between our house and Walt Whitman Middle School, where I would attend school in a few years.

I do not recall which one of us brought the matches, or whose idea it was to start a fire, but we decided to light a small fire. Young children rarely have experience with fires, so the concept that a little fire can become a big fire did not enter our heads. The fascination with the idea of burning things shuts down all functions of the brain.

It was windy when we lit our fire, which meant more air to feed the flames. The fire began to grow hotter and larger with all the oxygen it was receiving. The more oxygen, the better the combustion. We stood there frozen as we watched our fire spread to more and more leaves, not knowing how to stop it from growing. We abandoned all efforts to contain the blaze and ran like crazy.

Our hearts were pounding when we fled to the safety of our homes. I am surprised our mothers never asked why we were out of breath when we ran in the door. Although, our running in the front door for a snack or to use the bathroom was a common occurrence.

The fire department was called by one of the neighbors and saved the day. Fortunately for me, I did get to attend Walt Whitman instead of being sent to a school for juvenile delinquents. What lesson can we learn from our adventure of starting a small fire?

A Lesson To Learn: *Be Careful What You Say About Others*

"Where there is no wood, a fire goes out, and where there is no gossip, contention ceases." Proverbs 26:20 NET

Have you ever made fun of someone to your friends? Maybe someone irritated you and you wanted to complain about them? We have all talked about others in harmful ways when they were not around. Gossip is saying something about someone that may or may not be true. Ultimately it is hurtful and destructive to their reputation.

In the same way that our forest fire started with one match and a little pile of leaves and sticks, it is wrong to talk about someone in an unkind way - even just a little bit. Like my little fire, even small gossip usually leads to something bigger that can get out of control and hurt so many people, including the one who started it.

A Prayer To Pray: God help me be careful to only say things that build others and not to tear them down. Help me guard my heart from jealousy, anger, comparison, and unkind words. And, when I hear others gossiping, help me change the subject, say something positive, or leave. Thank You!

Adventure 22: June Bugs Make Good Kites

Kids can be highly creative and resourceful when it comes to making things on their own. Like most children, we built forts in our den out of pillows and sheets. Our little minds imagined pirates attacking us or fighting off armies. My parents graciously allowed us to rearrange the furniture if we put it back close to where it came from.

When I got older and we moved to Atlanta where we took fort-building to the next level, constructing tree houses in our backyard. My brother Kurt and I used scrap lumber from the new homes being built in our neighborhood to also erect elaborate tree houses in the woods.

When we lived in the Washington, DC. suburbs, each house had a large yard with lots of grass and clover. Nobody cared about having weeds growing in their yards when I was a kid. I have many fond memories of playing tag and hide and seek with my friends for hours in these yards. I distinctly remember the clover because the bees loved it. We usually played games barefoot in the grass which resulted in many a painful bee sting, but that did not stop us.

We had finished playing all the games we knew and were sitting on the grass in my backyard trying to think of something new to do to entertain ourselves. At this point my creative spirit came upon me. There were dozens of these crazy green beetles flying around our heads that hot August afternoon. I had an idea! We ran inside to find my mother's sewing box and got a spool of thread. We caught a June Bug and tied the thread to one of its six legs. Then, we let the June bug fly off. Of course, we held on to the thread and watched the June Bug fly around and around in circles over our heads. We had invented a new pastime! It was great fun for us kids!

I am not sure what the June Bug thought about his part in the exercise. They either got tired of flying and were released, or their leg pulled off and they earned their freedom. There was a never-ending supply of June Bugs, so we played with our new pets for hours.

A Lesson To Learn: *You Can Be Creative Like The One Who Created You*

"Then God said, "Let us make human beings in our image, to be like us. Us make man in Our image." Genesis 1:26

God created the earth – all the plants, animals, rivers, and oceans. He made the billions of stars, as well as every person who has ever lived. He also made you in His image with the ability to create things like I did when I tied the string on the June Bug's leg. Of course, that was simple and childlike. I was only 8 years old at the time. Now I create books for children like you to read. I have created artwork, built houses, and creatively raised 7 great children with my wife. God gave me the ability to design, build, and create things that I never imagined.

The same Creator wants to come and live in you and unleash your God-given creative spirit. You can express your creativity through art, music, science, writing, building - among many other ways. How have you been creative? Talk with your parents or grandparents about what you would like build, make, or create. Start with something simple and fun like tying a string on a June Bug.

Adventure 23: Sneaking Up On A Skunk

Deer hunting on David Greenwood's property in Maxeys, Georgia with my friends provided many hours of adventures, fellowship, and usually some venison to feed our families. It was great fun!

On this day, the deer had eluded us, so I left the woods empty handed. It was a moonless night and I could not see my hand in front of my face! I climbed down from my tree, turned on my flashlight, and walked up the hill. I enjoyed the sound of crunching as I walked on the dry fall leaves that littered the forest floor. I emerged out onto a large field of soft green grass that made my walking almost silent. I was happy I had a flashlight to see where I was going. The light drove away the shadows as well as my fear of the dark.

As I approached to the middle of the field, my flashlight ran across something moving slowly along the ground. Curious, I decided to walk closer to get a better look. It was so dark, that I found myself almost on top of the object before I realized what it was a... SKUNK! Oh no! I froze.

I remembered reading stories about people who had been sprayed by skunks. They had to throw their clothes away and could not get the foul odor off their body for days. All these thoughts raced through my mind, keeping pace with my racing heart. I dared not run and startle the little creature.

I decided to move very slowly away, praying that the skunk would remain calm as well. Could it hear my heart beating and my heavy breathing? Would I be able to escape? Look what trouble my curiosity had gotten me into!

Fortunately, I was able to slip away and avoid getting sprayed that night. I cannot imagine what I would have done if I had been doused, since we had a two-hour drive back home together in the truck! My friends may have insisted that I ride in the truck bed - even if it was cold outside!

A Lesson To Learn: *God Protects Us From Hidden Danger*

"It is He who reveals the profound and hidden things; He knows what is in the darkness, and the light dwells with Him." Daniel 2:22

The Lord will protect you from all evil; He will keep your soul. The Lord will guard your going out and your coming in from this time forth and forever." Psalm 121:7-8

There have been many times where God has protected me from something dangerous that I was not aware of at the time. The skunk could have sprayed me with its horrible smelly spray that fall evening. God knew the skunk was in the field and He protected me from the danger.

There are many times God has protected you from danger as well. He has kept you safe on the highways, safe from food poisoning, and even safe from bad people. He shows us dangerous situations so that we will get away from them, just like I slipped quietly away from the skunk when I realized I was in danger.

When God shows you something dangerous, often the best thing to do is to respond wisely by leaving. Sometimes it is best to run away from a harmful situation, even if your friends do not agree. Danger can come when you are surfing the web or when you are outside in nature as I was. Ask God to protect you. Here is a suggested prayer.

A Prayer To Pray: Dear God, please protect me from hidden danger. Help me when I see the danger to choose wisely, to run away so that I will not get hurt or hurt others. Help me to understand what is evil and give me the strength to say no to the temptation, even if my friends do not.

What To Do If You (Or Your Dog) Get Sprayed

Here is one effective way to get rid of the smell from the skunk spray. It can be used safely on your dog, cat, or even your dad when he comes home from hunting smelling like a skunk. Make sure there is an adult there to help you, as this can be dangerous.

Mix these ingredients:
1 quart of 3-percent hydrogen peroxide
1/4 cup baking soda
1 teaspoon liquid dish-washing soap

It is a good idea to wear rubber gloves when applying this solution to the victim. It is best to apply the solution immediately after being sprayed. Be careful protect the eyes. If you do not have peroxide, a mixture of baking soda, liquid dish soap, and diluted vinegar will word as well.

Do not mix this solution ahead of time or store it because the chemical reaction could cause the bottle to explode over time. Rub the mixture all over and scrub deep to neutralize the odor — however, if you are washing your dog or cat, do not leave the mixture on longer than you have to as peroxide can bleach fur. Rinse the solution off thoroughly, and the smell should be gone.

Adventure 24: Singing To A Doodlebug

Doodlebug is the name affectionately given to Ant Lion larva, tiny insects, that live in the ground right under our feet, especially if your feet are standing on sandy soil. You see, Doodlebugs prefer building their traps in sandy soil for a reason. A Doodlebug digs a little pit in the sand and then lays in the bottom of this pit covered up by the sand, waiting for ants to come along and fall in. Once the ant gets tired of trying to escape, they slide down to the bottom where the Doodlebug will catch them and eat them. It sounds like something out of a science fiction movie and they look the part as well!

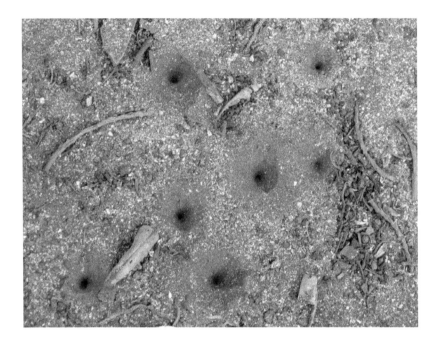

Our friends explained to us city kids how to locate and capture the little creatures. One of them got a little twig and slowly stirred the sand pit as we watched wide-eyed. Then, to our surprise, they started singing this song to get the Doodlebug to reveal himself.

Doodlebug, doodlebug,
Come out of your hole
Your house is on fire,
And your children will burn.

Wow! They were so serious about hunting for Doodlebugs that someone wrote a song for the ritual. They religiously sang the song every time they stirred the sand in a new pit. It must have worked, as the Doodlebug inevitably revealed himself and was caught with the child's fingers. Then they would hold the little creature on the palm of their hand like a prized trophy!

A Lesson To Learn: *The Spiritual World Is Unseen*

"We are not looking at what can be seen but at what cannot be seen. For what can be seen is temporary, but what cannot be seen is eternal."
2 Corinthians 4:18

In the same way that we could not see the Doodlebugs under the sand, we cannot see the spiritual world with our eyes. We were able to uncover the little Doodlebugs and hold them in our hands. Conversely, we are not able to touch God or other spiritual beings, but they are just as real as anything you can see or touch.

Jesus said this to His disciples after He came back from the dead, *"See My hands and My feet, that it is I Myself; touch Me and see, for a spirit does not have flesh and bones as you see that I have."* Luke 24:39

There are spiritual beings all around us. The good ones are called angels and the bad ones are called demons. God Himself is spirit and does not have a physical body. All of these beings are unseen, but they are alive and real.

You can learn how to see what is not seen by your eyes by reading the Bible and praying - talking with God. Ask God to reveal Himself to you, to speak to you, and to change your life. Ask Him to reveal His love and salvation to your friends who do not know Him yet. Ask Him to use you to explain the Good News of Jesus to them.

A Prayer To Pray: God, please help me have better vision – to see the eternal, to see the spiritual things going on around me. Help my family and friends to see You living in me and come to know you as I have. Speak to their hearts and show them Your love for them in the person of Jesus Christ.

Granddad's Final Thoughts

In the beginning of this book, I described how God has revealed Himself to me through His creation. Each of my animal adventures was an encounter with one of His creatures and was therefore an encounter with Him.

I hope, now that you are finished reading my book, that God has revealed Himself to you as well. He loves you so much and desires a personal relationship with you. The most powerful way that God has revealed Himself to you was through His Son - Jesus Christ.

"But now in these days He has spoken to us through His Son to whom He has given everything and through whom He made the world and everything there is." Hebrews 1:2 TLB

Remember, God is looking for you! I pray that you will look for Him and find Him.

> *"If you look for Me wholeheartedly, you will find Me."* Jeremiah 29:13 NLT

Your friend in the adventure,

Granddad Steve
secureingod@gmail.com

Granddad Steve's First Book

Granddad Steve's first book, Secure In An Insecure World, was written primarily for singles to help them make a wise decision about who they marry. It addresses our natural insecurity, loneliness, and the cultural pressure that often motivate us to get married. These can make us desperate, leading to a poor decision. Steve's book helps the reader understand how to live content and secure in God's love before they marry. Over the years, Steve's book has also helped married couples live content and secure in God and His love which has empowered them to love one another as never before.

Secure In An Insecure World was first published in 2008 in Kiev, Ukraine, where Steve and Danelle served as missionaries at the time. It has since been translated into Russian and Spanish. You can find hard copies or e-books in English or Spanish on any of these sites:

Amazon: http://tinyurl.com/qjv8963 (English)
http://tinyurl.com/gnfr6xm (Spanish)

The book is also available as an e-book on:
Kindle: http://15th.stRDd52i/
IPad: http://15th.st/k5DtuK
Nook: http:15th.st/kXrAV

Photo Credits

CPSIA information can be obtained
at www.ICGtesting.com
Printed in the USA
BVHW020620121120
593099BV00010B/101